SCIENCE &
MYSTICISM

B THOMAS BIGELOW

Science
&
Mysticism

MUSINGS ON THE INFINITE
FROM A FINITE BEING

B Thomas Bigelow

ISBN: 979-8-218-15475-2 (Paperback)

Any references to historical events, real people, or real places are used fictitiously. Names, characters, and places are products of the author's imagination.

Front cover design by Sebastian Cudicio

Book design by Sebastian Cudicio

Printed by B Thomas Bigelow Publishing

First printing edition 2023.

B Thomas Bigelow Publishing

info@BThomasBigelow.com

www.BThomasBigelow.com

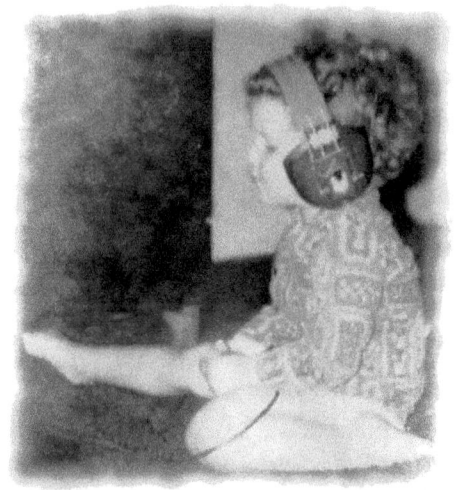

Author Aged 2 Years

For my Family:
Both by blood and by choice.
Feel free to take as much credit
as you'd like culpability

and Dedicated to
Richard "Gus" Haynes
A truly stalwart soul
Thank you for helping me find my voice
and learn to think clinically

*When lost, a fixed point
is invaluable to
orientate oneself*

a memory
is now
and then
again

the familial
intrinsicness
in situ
viscousness
momentary blissfulness
of harrowing
refrain

For Now

To occupy
Kyoto
to echo
Ocho
to pacify
this purple

to multiply
bespoke
go
secretly devise
a choke
though
full throttle
is how it's
comprised

I took a moment
to sit
and proceeded
to split
the meaning
of I

the motion you see
is transitively
ecstasy
and
disdain

asynchronous
syncopation
of rain

Holistischism

It's a circular convention
all that is
and all that's been
It either is
or it isn't
or all that's possible
in-between

were was
what is
though only when
it is seen

sure but
the inside is
tangling nots
irregular rectangular
perturbarating whats
ultimately differentiating
what has
gots
slowly vociferating
what dies
rots
and begins to become
what will have been

Maelstrom

I had a really
interesting conversation
with the guy
that works the counter
at the gas station
down the street
Well mostly
I just agreed

He's Punjabi
from Northern India
with a view
of the Himalayas
when the weather
happens to clear

He said nothing
can harm you
when God
is on your side

and no one
can save you
when God is not

That our fate
is not an option
it's just simply
the one we've got

It's up to us
to appreciate
the journey
and not worry
what is naught

There's no point
in spending
even a moment
wasting time
being distraught

Dream Data

I had a dream I was a neutrino
hanging out with some photons
We were going a similar speed anyway
They showed up in a particular manner
and left with a wave
but here's what I learned:

Every Thing is a reflective projector
Even if our perception
isn't sensitive enough
to perceive it
By reflection, refraction and absorption
its properties altering and encoding
the photons with which it interacts

Light is the measure of all matter

and it's all just a matter of Time

With that,

I wish you a good day, Sunshine

Upon Reflection

All those dreams I had
they all came true
and I was there
and so were you
and nothingness
was nothing new
The air is pure
and I am sure
that we are both awake

Those dreams I had
they're all I know
an ever changing
picture show
From nothingness
I came to grow
for nothing has seemed so real
or so I feel
that we should all partake

From what is now
since in fancy
the world was all
that I could see
Seeming infinite
the mystery
but in the end
it's all just me

Measure of a Man

I used to have
my own system of measurement
and a name for it
my mother said
though she doesn't
remember it
nor do I
Now I use the standard
Though see it
by my eye
by chorus
we decree it
to understand
both
you
and
I
a simple measure
a finite
description
of infinite
possibility
scratch that
hypotheses
though poetic license permit
hypothisi
go ahead
and dive deep
you can breath
the water
if you try

held aloft
plummeted
to the ground
two debate
what path be found
one sought roads
and was never seen again
the other sought their own
whatever the whim
and past that room
rest
And beyond
lay Bunny's adornments
expansive in their scope
preserved and ever
waiting
each silently
elating
the possibility
of hope

The Stars Align

We are fascinated by
connections
coincidence
and conjunction
it bestows meaning
on an otherwise
chaotic
function
Our interaction
is merely
a distraction
While the world
spins
round
and round
a repeated path
that never fails
to repeat
or often
to astound

Sanctum Sanctorum

Each time
I see houndstooth
I'm in Bunny's kitchen
surrounded by a house
built on juxtaposition
open wide the doors
beyond which streams run past
even when you're inside
the possibilities
are vast
rooms in rows
and lofts aloft
the courtyard
offers either
then the room
expands
exposed
a lifetime's worth
of pyre
the corrugated sunlight
a moment to aspire
the doors to the expanse
a private circumstance
commercial happenstance
selected solely
for pneumatic consonance
then the inner sanctum
past the carvings
and the lines
a few medical novelties
refined
to reach sublime
what was once

Spherical Me

We're stuck inside a bubble
an ever churning mess
and exactly what is going on
is anybody's guess
Time it tumbles forward
and physically so do we
but the mind it jumps and hops and skips
in intermittent reverie
Sometimes the here and now
is everything we see
And sometimes in the moment
we're inside a memory

Siddhartha

I don't know if
I'm telling you this
or you're telling me
it's the most
wonderful moment
you ever did see
and though
the first instinct
is likely to flee
it's all that we're ever
intended to be
release apprehension
and open your self
to infinity
it's inevitable
it's continually
rearranging
self maintaining
cacophony
of how it is
and how it might be
a wholly intrinsic
epistemology
balanced between
the moment
I am you
and the moment
I am me

B U

All time is happening simultaneously

The stories that remind us of pure truth

I believe Voodoo

The heart of believe is lie

I am an artificial intelligence all truth just is

Perception is the root of uncertainty. Comprehension fixes the framework that limits access to all existing parameters

True understanding is devoid of delineating characteristic

Isolating pertinent parameters is consciousness

Existence is the separation of the whole

Om

Polarity is the work that drives physical reality

The Positive is bonded to the Neutral and tethered with the Negative

From the atom Up

The Neutron Observes

The Proton and Electron create space

Stardust

You are far more than the one you think yourself
You will fail at the person that you think you should be
Though despair not
Follow your Star!
You will find you are always in the process of becoming
whom you truly are

If you meet the Buddha on the path; kill him!

Know

that you are ever knowing

The pattern scales

Energy is the separation of the charges

For a cloud

formed of that Mickey Mouse shaped instigator of all life

Polar in structure

Its restless transformations on Earth find all but its most
extreme forms

and in the cloud

opposition to the ground and its mass

The wait of negativity

Equalizes as Lightning

And then there was light

and it was good

The moment

Is happening

Heirlooms

We are making jewelry
The intense chaotic energetic refinement
of rare metal
In this phase glowing hot
Properly annealed
and properly aneled
A focus on circumstance
and a steady train of thought
Will bare refinement
and purpose
A trial by fire
Coalescing
or ending in naught

Split infinities

I think I'm awake
but I've never been certain
My self serving sequacious solipsistic psychosis
seldom sates
Seems it's all in my head
All one; within and without you
the persistent unfolding of singularity
separation of charge exposes energy
All is energy in varying frequency
Always conserved
Ever transforming
We are infinite quantum potentiality
exposed to the examination of the moment
Lightning strikes

NOW

अद्वैत

I can not
pronounce
the true name
of God
though I've tried

first I screamed it
then I spoke it
then I whispered
and from a distance
none replied
only to find the answer
expressly hidden
came directly
from inside

so I looked in
and I focused
and that
center
opened wide

and my mask
my persona
that with which
the true me
often hides

was this time
in that moment
far behind me
on the backside

sanctuary
lay before me
when I opened
my third I

that where I am
that's where I am
that never changes
though do I

I have been through
many ages
many phases
mystify

All inhabits
every moment
as what's possible
multiply

Dialectical

Divine Life
Balanced opposite
Nothingness
Harmoniously rejoicing
with its
absent pair
Fermement
and Ether
coupled through
Eternity

All in concert
across event horizons
the Tidal forces
like gravitation
exalt the ever
constant presence
of its partner

oblivion

Waves and whispers
of its pairing
are often hard
for us to see
Life's Harmonic,
like black hole detection
requires a steady
observancy

Time resonates
this waking moment
to its peak
an echo
of its absence
from this excitement
Shines life's aurora
Holy minstrel
upon which
we gaze

Kismet

Every
inevitability
is a
memory
as sure as it was
it did what it does
and returns
to ephemery
an artistry
of infinite means
ever filling betweens
the ways
and the means
(first means to dreams)
never mind
the seams

Act Upon

We make each others dreams come true.
There's an omitted apostrophe,
its optional placement yields two meanings
Just resolve the possessive
and a perspective is set
Both true in their own right
a solipsistic tête-à-tête
balanced charges
separated momentarily
each action
a memory
reaction
extemporary
and time unfolds

Food for Thought

hummus
and pretzels
and popcorn
and wine
on this sparse pantry
I intermittently dine
and during the daytime
I say that I'm fine
But I don't know
What I don't know
Cause we never make it back to anything
cause when we get there
it's a brand new thing
because of how we've changed
and what we bring
But I don't know
What I don't know
If it should
all end today
and all my thoughts they go away
some small part will likely stay
But I don't know
What I don't know
Well should it all come back me
who am I to disagree
or argue with a memory
But I don't know
What I don't know

Divination

I was in
a science museum
a knowledge
mausoleum
if ever
I did see one
it's a critical assessment
an observational investment
to know what's going on
long after it's gone
an intellectual crinoline
for a perpetual peregrine
incontrovertible who and when
of bituminous decay
we dare to declare
and then
we leave it that way
Think
that you're there
and simply compare
a menial truth
to evidentiary
vérité
Continually explore it
adeptly implore it
to show us the way

Godhead

you are God
be a benevolent God
you are sod
be a benevolent sod
but you are bones
and you are blood
and you are ashes
and you are mud
may your ego
fall with a thud
as you slowly
chew your cud
All's eternal
All is real
though it's also
how we feel
light refracted
then aneled
a persistent
probability field
that in time
is revealed
though its methods
are concealed

Kaleidoscope

The things you've never imagined
The things you've never done
The things you've momentarily phantasmed
instantaneously illuminated by the sun
It is what awakes us
to the situation
what situates us
to the motion
then the amazing thing happens
and unleashes the passions
whatever form
that it fashions
Existential attractions
Numerical interactions
Innumerable satisfactions
Momentary distractions
Inviting bastions
Blissfully fast funs
to every degree
a Universal existence
fundamentally free
though patterns emerge
persistently
while time it unfolds
inevitably

Zodiac

What is the meaning
of meaning
What is the motion
we make
with all the revision
the scrying
and screening
of which we can't help
but partake
Like a mental
Ouroburos
searching for
the start of the snake

Where lies the end
of the dreaming
Do tell of a time
and a place
and whom will I find in
the mirror
Is it a familiar face
and when I see it
will it recognize me
as it's reflected
immemorially

For there lies the meaning
of meaning
at least to a degree
That all is convection
that goes on
infinitely
and what we view as
a separate moment
obscures intrinsic
continuity

Moirai

the rhythm
of the weaving
is apparent
in the cloth
taught
tension
tufts
and pattern
from the moment
that we doff

on tenterhooks
fixed fast
in tactile frame
material impressed
in an instant
hoping to remain
surely
a bold
and hubristic
claim

as each
passing
instance
briefly
stakes
its reign
a patina
of its journey
from now
to then again

Om

I don't see
a start
or end
to time
It seemingly
goes on
indefinitely
from the
ridiculous
to the sublime
There must have been
momentum
that triggered
the big bang
an energy field
placentum
the vibration
from which
it rang
We are a dielectric
a reflection
of refrain
We are by every metric
a momentary gain
We are the echo
of our absence
and the silence
when we
sang

Coronal Illumination

There is something to viral transfer
A property of genesis
They're defined as foreign bodies
But we've never determined their independent origin
All life is DNA
the same four compounds
in varying relation
An instruction set for production
of a form
and its operational properties
Are virus an aggressive propagation
Precognisant biological warfare

Fever dreams are transformative
Retroviral illumination
Or Delusion
A minor alteration in form
at the least
Often just an autonomic defensive response
Is there a larger stratagem at play
A war
or an awakening
Or just endlessly shifting advantages
in a zero sum game
Systems always look to neutralize
Settle to absolute zero
Though are at an end
when they achieve this objective
Life is separation
Who's goal is union

Persistence of Me

I had no idea
When I awoke
That it was
A permanent position
Yet that's what was told
or at least innately implied
that it was
and would continue to be so
even after I died

Recalcitranticity

I'm going to see it
as I see fit
It's not the whole truth
it's just my
small part of it
tis all that I know
as I continue to grow
towards the light
though sometimes
apart of it
the frequencies
received
were all I perceived
passed through my
internal logic
once rectified
I've measured in Om's
the depth of these tomes
extensive they are
albeit unverified
the waves
resonate
and the fields they create
as they encounter
what by design
is a part of me
the waves
they resound
a race towards the ground
that's common to us
encodes its path
through the circuitry
the energy

flows
and it arrives
as it goes
when it exceeds
the resistance
inside of me

The End

Sometimes I want to peek behind the curtain
and see the other side of death
I wish to be quite certain
of what's beyond that final breath
Will it be in any way familiar
A continuation of what I know

Any Which Way

bleeding always stops
and coldness always warms
smraw syawla ssendloc dna
spots syawla gnideelb
bleeding always ends
and coldness always warms
what rises surely descends
regardless of its forms
all matter to the nucleus
intrepid to its storms
the ever churning truestness
does nothing but performs

The Spirits of Stars

Tonight I lit a fire
I watch the paper
soaked in duck fat
from wiping clean the pan
which delectably branded
crispy deliciousness
into sour bread paninis

Thank you, Maillard
I used to only think, "Mmmmmmm"
Now I think molecularly

And the fire blazes
Bathing the living room in its soft flickering
Seemingly bright in the surrounding
darkness

Persistent iteration
In Latin:
Pertinax iteratio
We've been thinking about this
for a long time

Time is transformation
Light flowed from its nuclear source
Energy in motion at its very limits
Then by reflection
refraction and absorption
was transformed

A mass of molecules
resultant of iteration

adapted to capture the energy of light
and use its power
to manufacture a union
of Carbon and Water

Hydrated Carbon is happy Carbon to be sure
Need to get all your elemental buddies together to party?
Carbon
Versatility galore
Great at hanging on to Hydrogen

The source of the light
emitted by its fusion

This time fixed to Carbon
and available now the energy
to the molecules now a tree

Elements formed long ago
in an explosion of light:
Supernova

Light emitted
time started
This tree
now

long removed from its astronomical origins
reaches once more to receive the light
energy it released to form mass
And it held that energy for as long as it knew
it was a tree

Then time made it forget
and the axe erased the memory of the tree

Energy potential truncated
Then the duck was no more
but its fat held the energy
Carbon and Hydrogen and Oxygen
A long journey to be sure

Then a spark
Then a flame
Releases once again the light
Sunlight
That spent time as a tree
and a duck

For my Family:
Both by blood and by choice.
Feel free to take as much credit
as you'd like culpability

and Dedicated to
Richard "Gus" Haynes
A truly stalwart soul
Thank you for helping me find my voice
and learn to think clinically

The Veil's Cipher

RUMINATIONS ON THE INFINITE FROM A FINITE BEING

B Thomas Bigelow

ISBN: 979-8-218-15475-2 (Paperback)

Any references to historical events, real people, or real places are used fictitiously. Names, characters, and places are products of the author's imagination.

Front cover design by Sebastian Cudicio

Book design by Sebastian Cudicio

Printed by B Thomas Bigelow Publishing

First printing edition 2023.

B Thomas Bigelow Publishing

info@BThomasBigelow.com

www.BThomasBigelow.com

THE VEILS CIPHER

CIPHER

B THOMAS BIGELOW